KARA VENUS

Harper
and her
Dogs

A tale about introducing your fur-babies to your new baby

Harper's parents were thrilled to learn they would be bringing home a baby.

They had been only children for years!

They showed the dogs the stroller.

They showed them the car seat.

They showed them baby blankets and clothes!

Then they hoped
for the best.

Then came the day when Harper
was born.

The fur babies were left with
Grandma and Grandpa.

When Harper came inside,
her parents were hesitant.

To their surprise, they fell in love!

They cleaned up her messes.

They played together.

They became her protector.

They became her best friend.